In the Tree Where the
Double Sex Sleeps

Winner of the Iowa Poetry Prize

In the Tree Where the
Double Sex Sleeps

Rob Schlegel

University of Iowa Press · Iowa City

University of Iowa Press, Iowa City 52242
Copyright © 2019 Rob Schlegel
www.uipress.uiowa.edu
Printed in the United States of America
Design by Sara T. Sauers

The University of Iowa Press is a member of Green Press
Initiative and is committed to preserving natural resources.
Printed on acid-free paper

Library of Congress Cataloging-in-Publication Data
Names: Schlegel, Rob, author.
Title: In the tree where the double sex sleeps / Rob Schlegel.
Description: Iowa City : University of Iowa Press, 2019. |
Series: Iowa Poetry Prize |
Identifiers: LCCN 2018040183 (print) | LCCN 2018042138
(ebook) | ISBN 978-1-60938-646-7 (ebook) |
ISBN 978-1-60938-645-0 (pbk. : acid-free paper)
Classification: LCC PS3619.C424 (ebook) |
LCC PS3619.C424 A6 2019 (print) | DDC 811/.6—dc23
LC record available at https://lccn.loc.gov/2018040183

For Wil
&
Linden Mae

There's wood enough within.

CALIBAN, in Shakespeare's
The Tempest, act 1, sc. 2

CONTENTS

In the Tree Where the
Double Sex Sleeps

I.

Show Cave

It begins with hide and seek in the cave spring air warms.
Why, even the dogwoods shed blossoms
over the dead sculpture garden
where the oracle speaks on behalf of the gods.

Near the fountain, a few deer, rich with insides
different from mine, but the same,
incorporated as I am, though wired to nothing.

I fold leaves into swans. Rearrange the trees.
The oracle touches my face.
Language is where you live in mere fidelity to narrative, she says.

But language is not my first language.

Novella

1.

What grows in my throat fits so well I can breathe, but not eat.
Acorn, or wild apple, says the doctor.
Quince, or egg of quail, says mother.

Father draws on the wall a series of lines becoming letters.
Or are they leaves? How long do I have,
I ask. But the doctor
is sand. I step into father's forms. Mother's gaze
keeps me warm.

I blow stones at birds in towers. They rain down on me.
Make me feel like fainting.

I lead a calf into the barn, set to work
beating it. I seal the windows
for nine days. On the tenth, the barn is full of bees
crowded in clusters roiling over each other.

One emerges from the calf's mouth
and transforms into an owl.

Cursed child, it says,
one day you will kill your mother and father.

2.

In the garden, mother cuts daisies, fingers a leaf from her hair.

On my face, a panic I can't talk my way through
because the owl made a nest in my dry mouth.

For days I fight against obsessing over the owl's prophecy.
I've a mind to wander,
to never see mother and father again.

The owl calls my name; scary
male flower. The edges of her mouth, cracked and bleeding.

Ice in my bones, she says.

I press my hands around her body. When she stops shaking,
I fall asleep.

3.

I'm on a stage before an audience comprised
of everyone I've ever known.
Behind me a dread glare shines so brightly, one by one
the audience leaves.

I look out over the empty seats, the wall's dim sconces
illuminate paintings of water plants wavering in a temper of plumes.

I think childhood was pretty good sometimes—
father opening the blinds
because he knew the morning light would flood the room.

4.

I clean the cavities of shot birds.
Sun spreads blood in the sky, opening
into an isle full of noise, airs, delights
and mirrors turning. Children bury children
under piles of leaves. One of them
turns to me. Mother and father to the bee barn, she says.

I walk into the night. Impulse turns over my mind.
I smell my hands. Owl. Grape vine.

Rain fills the gridded sky. My careful inner forecast is light
noise passing for tragedy.

In a letter home I write: Dear mother, dear father:
such violent forces. The children's
voices. I talk to my doctor, but forget
his orders. Am I candle boy?
Attic shape? To leave the circle of my mistakes
I walk to the abandoned church,
ring the bell in the tower, hang on the rope
with all my weight. Feel myself borne up in its flight.

5.

Balls of neon light quiver like nerve fibers spilled
from the nape of a human neck.

My applause masks the terror of thinking I've seen this before.
I climb a ladder to a parking garage,
open my mouth wider than necessary
and close my teeth on a shiny coin.

Afraid the cameras are making me real,
I walk the spiral stairs through an attic onto a roof
whose water tower I scale into an apartment filled with dragon trees,
reading chairs, floor lamps casting ovals of light.
I could live here, I think, then shut my eyes
over another crackle of spine light.

Every hour takes figuring out how to live again.

Navigating the next flight of stairs steeper than the last,
I realize ascent is the wrong way out. I stop halfway, spit the coin,
and finally call out for help.

6.

I wake on the hour. No idea where I am, which year of my life.

Am I really the person mother says
and not the irregular triangle of sheep flocking uphill?

Father kills a fish in such a way
there grows in me a song I am enlivened by,
enough to eat the food on my plate.

Mother points at whales breaching in the sound.
My mind is almost mine again. I should do something—
help my parents pull beets before dark.
But I just sit there, watching rain turn the sound into stone.

7.

Why are you grieving?

Because the others are grieving.

You are not compelled to grieve independently?

The grass needs raking.

The grass?

The leaves. I'll build a fence to keep them from the sea.

Then will you help the others?

Tollers ring bells even the dead can hear,
a ringing such that I am bound to.

And the leaves?

When they are taken by the waves I give them names,
desiring in this act
a homecoming I'm constantly denied
on account of the owl's prophecy.

8.

I wake to a wolf sniffing my groin.
Sister Wolf, I say, be slow. Do no harm, and I'll provide you
a lifetime of live feed, and a finger to point with.

When I leave to find a herd, I can't help but return to the bee barn.
Small holes open in my palms.
I feather my sarong. Sister Gardener plucks it. I create a border.
Brother Dermis maintains it.

Trees push up through particles of air
then down through the ground with equal force.

Artifice one way. Authenticity the other.

I pull on my cloak, a remoteness even Sister Virus envies.

I pass the time in the barn wondering what might become of me
if those I loved knew the extent of my love.

Sister Wolf visits weekly. I confess
nothing. She says mother and father are wearing paths
into the ground with their pacing.

Citrus Cell

A child whose name I can't say sits beneath the lemon tree.

Silt-clouds billow under fish
thinking with their skin
in the pond around which
paths for the occult
are hardly visible under rival strains of ivy.

What did you see, little fish? Clock turns from 3:33
to death wish to the lemon tree.

The waves are all of history in a moment.

Moses, throw down your staff, and lo
it's a serpent. Put your hand inside
your coat, and behold, it is flesh.

Lydia, Lydia, Tuesday, Rocket are the names
of my daughter's make-believe horses. I taste the lemon,
but break the tree.

Does the lemon taste me?

Nature Breeds a Promise-Keeping Animal

Pointing to the dead rabbit, my daughter says, Rock.
Dogs circle dirt where murder wore
the grass away. Absolute
arrangement on Lewis Street.

Wind ruins the volunteer maples near the lake
through which I'm free to wade,
watching my daughter on shore drawing circles on paper,
mindful of the white space.

A different kind of freedom
is throwing rocks
into the lake and knowing the lake's response.

The Animal That Therefore I Am

How dead my face must look from inside
this screen. The internet
explains paintings to me.

I dream what these paintings
want me to dream.
The next sentence pretends relevance

to an animal future. What can I do
with this material called
Real? When I walk through caves of raspberry cane

I think I think I'm more alive than I feel.

Flesh Turns Stone into Music

Dinner is yellow beets, lettuce, and beer.
Whose plates are these?

Tonight, the dead are everywhere.

I ask the words that remain—winter, symphony,
delusion—what, if anything, I should say.

I whisper the names of those
who did not die in their sleep,
but the other way. To sound
a body out; one-part pinion, one-part
mouth, from which I hang
death masks on a branch in the linden.

Birds flit in and out of the eyes. These are the sounds
I'll remember them by.

The Forested Sea

Thin as the air carrying the arrow
to your favorite animal's neck

woodswallows nest in a tree
adorned with drawings of trees

the lines of which are worn faint
from the hands of the dying.

Grant them the blood of your attention.
They're ready to speak.

II.

Early Onset

I can hear the hiss of dazed insects
pressed between pages of *Spiritual Experience*.
All these gulls in their duress
over the boy washed against rocks
rich with berries hawthorns drop.

There's the sailor holding my ticket away
from love's cut I can't see because of the prophecy.

The owl's vacant eye appears
more vacant inside the Museum of Natural History.
Hex on the ship is never enough.

Eyes damned in the near work, red and tender.
There's the oracle.
We meet as though we've never met
the poem's void under the shadow of swords.

Clamor the Bells Falling Bells

1.

All day, the moody air. After lunch, I dress like Lear,
stand opposite Hannah, playing Goneril.
Two crowns on the table. I choose Goneril's.

Fine, the director says, but read Lear's lines.

Hear, nature, hear: dear goddess . . .
Into her womb convey sterility.
Dry up in her the organs of increase . . . If she must teem,
create her child of spleen . . .

Goneril winces. Or is it Hannah; a living father's living daughter . . .

Blindfolded, I'm led downstage.
Extemporize on the word "vision" the director says.

I talk about Edgar's imagination nurturing Gloucester,
until Gloucester finally sees
beyond his false fall over the cliffs of Dover.

The director removes the blindfold. My eyes squint
into a spotlight's glare.

Is nudity standing on a stage, pretending to be someone else,
or standing on a stage, pretending to be yourself?

2.

On my way home, lightning strobes
the neighborhood. I open the door to the house
so dark is it even a house?

As children, my sister and I battled for control
of the TV. Fingernails
dug into my arm. When I kicked her in the groin
she collapsed to the floor.

I enter the children's room. Boy body. Girl body.
Breathing sleep they sound the same.

3.

The next morning, Lindy points out the window.
A strand of gossamer
floats near the roofline. Then another,
and another. Hundreds of barely visible spinnerets
drift through the air.

4.

I watch a killdeer run, panicked over the grass.
It's pretending to be wounded,
that it might draw my attention away from its nest.

Beyond the fence, Wil is on his knees.
For a moment, I think he's praying
but he's planting flowers
around the base of the flagpole
marking the distance between me
and the disaster of ignoring my intuition.

One thing I love about Kisha
is that she never stops me from staring at men
I hope see in me what I see in them.

5.

Every fall, baby spiders climb to a high point,
position their abdomen to the sky
and release fine silk spinnerets
until the slightest breeze carries them away.

The spiders travel a few feet, or a thousand miles.
The migration is called
ballooning. Mortality is high.

6.

We're eating crêpes suzette. Jellies cool in jars.
What remains of the lightning
is needles. Kids chalk the sidewalk
with words: friendship; courage; honesty; work.

I trap a daddy longlegs in my glass.
Search my phone for facts.

That beautiful couple's argument is enhanced
by a busker's violin conspiring against loneliness.

Daddy longlegs have no spinnerets.

7.

Owls mock the strawberry moon. That's my cue.

Another "e" in red makes the word
more liquid, like vowels I lower
my throat into. They say you can hide
your daughtered mind, but you can't
uproot the mandrake; the sound alone
kills you faster than the crown.

White brick deflects the sun warming . . .
what is it? Lavender I turn
into love, skirting waves. I smooth my shirt,
enter the house with a potted mandrake.

The meaning I'm trying to protect is
the heart is neither boy, nor girl. I close my hand
around the stem and pull.

Essay on the Nature and Principles of Air

I wore a dress to the funeral

I ate a cake

A slice of cake

A cake

A slice of cake

My summary is: the whole cake

.

The house could be a prison,
but it's religion, personal history, paranoia's
triangle-shaped pond

.

Mother, how do you know me

By your soup

Searches

Why do I cry after sex

Can I eat old chocolate

Will juniper berries make me crazy

Can I really eat breakfast at Tiffany's

What if an asteroid

What if a Metroid

How do moons sex

Does bonsai sex

Is it true you don't choose who you love

What does Sugar say

What says *Genesis*

O brave little engine

Where is your aorta

Am I addicted quiz

Can I take my dog's Tryptanol

Can I buy a house with a credit card

How does Nike fuck

Was John Ashbery

When did Reagan walk the earth

Can I deep-fry Dayquil

O brave little engine

Where is your pituitary

What if my toddler ate my Zoloft

Is it okay to take pictures at a wake

When should I give my therapist a gift

Is it normal for cats to pant

What are symptoms of candida

How does Sony fuck

Does the internet make me depressed

Is it okay the police

Does America own the moon

O brave little engine

Where are your ovaries

Does gravity bend light

Can I eat Lucifer's wife, and what wonders is she sitting on, over there

Do my coworkers like me quiz

What if I were famous vine

Is my son's Vader helmet more vitally alive when it's in the closet,
no longer reduced to the context in which it was made

How does the cloud fuck

What if Brandon was a dinosaur

What if Dot was a sea cucumber

What if America's Dad

What if I was a girl

Is intuition good or bad

Will I die before my children

Is glass even a thing

A falling stone endeavors to continue in its motion

What if a bullet

Is brain future proof

When am I going to feel okay

Are you there, it's me, Robbie

How does this phone work

How do you know

Fable on Lunar Formation

I know a place, the man says, where we can escape these dangerous conditions. Walls in the house are Kyoto green. This is yours, he says, then steps from a cliff into the sea. I know a place, the woman says, where we can escape these dangerous conditions. We arrive at the mouth of the cave. This is yours, she says, then disappears down a narrow passage. The next day, I walk amidst burnt trees. A deer crosses in front of me. I follow through timber, charred, and thinning to meadow. The deer stops but says nothing of the moon's first hour.

Interrogative

Dogs bark the sun down. The oracle speaks.

What ideas come into your head?
What spiritual experiences?

Music's superiority is its absence of reason.

You yell at your children . . .

After seeing pictures of friends at parties
I can be a little reactionary.

Your children call you "Poppy."

The first time I touched the ocean
my mother warned, Careful, Robbie, the waves
don't know what they are.

III.

Le Soi

Be lost! or just
Be you, Kisha says the morning spiders trigger the smoke alarm
Panic retails for the change I throw away
When the pledge of allegiance is frozen
    Verse
In conflict with where I live in relation to labor blistering hands
In fields spring rains erode. I know you know
What I mean when I say I want
    A Mary face. Life's less
Reaffirming. Wil's teacher teaches division via word problem.
Jake cuts his pie into six pieces. That some students
Don't know what pie is is
    American as
Maybe I'll spend my gap year in D.C. massaging ocean policy.
When I'm mercury, I read *Frankenstein*. Moon to me; cube to boys
    Coding malware. Mary
Shelley learned to write her name by tracing it
From her mother's grave. What I love about mom is
Your trauma is my trauma. In daydream, I tell Picasso, Nice portrait
    Of Gertrude. Yes, he says, everybody says
She does not look like it. When I'm with you, you're with what
You think is me: husband of a genius
    Whose prose makes you weep. When I'm alcohol I sound
My god. Care with words is one form of control. When I'm field
The fox sleeps. I impress my sisters when I'm silk.

Firewall

As a father who wishes to be a mother,
I come as I am to the party,
my hand over the scar marking the distance
between knowing and telling.

I'm nothing but the games I play against
despair, paternal and discursive,
as if the scar might disappear were I less
pregnant with me turning air into fear.

Gethsemane

The children need space. One hits the other.

The wireless breaks, opens
to the street's
beings toward death.

What worked for them
might work for me—
sentences, friends
so ritualistic, they are their own ritual

•

My daughter says she'll break
my blood. I look her
in the eye. She's stronger than me

•

Am I ever myself to myself, if I'm not merely
remembering myself

is how you see the cedar

By you, I mean me, further in

Threat Perception

1.

I touch my face performing language the children freeze.

Time we make for each other
is when I say to Kisha,
What I'm feeling is business-casual
for therapists like Alice,
cure to the woe I am signing Square.

If the first person to think humanly
invented gods out of fear, is fear the science I need?

I pay Alice to listen. Ellen to cut my hair. Kisha, nothing.
How out of line
the ocean is. My threshold for its effects
touch my face, a softer he.

2.

Safeway's a total bust. They sell the deadest meat.
I end up spending way too much
on salmon smoked industrially.

Lindy's down the aisle, calling for me.
Poppy, are you hiding? Greens wilt into greens
misters crisp to fresh. What fiction.

Fingers in mint I mistake for rosemary.
What aisle is this? Forecast calls for blow—
someone else's turn to care; that dad melting brie
in the marvelous glitter of his mouth.

3.

Is air evidence, or virus I worry toward likely?
I'd ask Alice, but she's in Rome.

Through December the Academy screens
Home Alone. Mandarins
on the table mold. I give one to Lindy
I don't wish ill, I just worry
worrying's death winning in absentia.

Cough a mole. Are you good?

On the bus, a pool of blood makes gossip shapes
a stranger's body spilled
like life I drag a shoelace through.

4.

The night raspberries enchant the table
I give up trying to name a pure substance.
Everything's made of something else

which is fashion, like sunset when evening brings
no prayer, save,
Save me. I'm where I shouldn't be.

I'm not my hair, nor this *Portable Emerson.*
How I feel is what I see. Flesh lights the room
cooled by ferns cats probe.

Surveillance Face is the portrait of the poet
cleaning his mouth with prose.

The ferns? Fake. I'm bad at loving, aging, being
complex; code for:

5.

If only I could stand on my head between mirrors,
trace one hand with the other,
the horror of it, like an animal, or worse
an animal I know.

6.

Wil and I paint our fingernails.
I know a Nietzsche scholar
who also paints his nails, I say.
Wil's face twists into a dried apricot,
as if warning, Don't realize me,
or we might tumble together, depersonalized.

Let us treat each other well
as if we are real; perhaps we are

I want to say

even as I fear for him, that all his life
he'll walk alone
into the flames of a singular rage.

7.

Life forks into countless futures. In one of them
Wil and the serpent inside him
are my enemies. The serpent bites, spits bile
in fits and elbows
flying, and words promising
worse. I tell Wil I can remove the serpent
by means of a harmless purge.

He lies on his back. Shuts his eyes.
I rub his stomach until his skin burns;
illusion turned upon itself, opening into the real.

The serpent's in me, not Wil.

8.

I subdue the overwhelming sublime by writing
prose between mirrors accentuating

blemishes made worse by my imperfect mouth
Kisha promises to kiss when I offer it.

Forgive me for staring, but your waist is so . . .
so Victorian.

After reading Ruskin we make love in shirts
whose arms we knot for less control.

In the morning, it's like angels really are
and not merely episodic bells against dying.

9.

In the kitchen, I rinse something red from my hair.
Wil enters with spiders
a nightmare left in his mouth.

My eyes grow to see you, he says.
I hate his knowing so much before reason intervenes.

I feel better after reading,
Poets are ludicrous and the best people I know, in Callie's poem.

Wil draws a serpent that will die soon. The serpent
stares at me until I change.

10.

On the phone with his grandfather,
Wil describes his day. I look for myself in every word.
I never want to exist outside his thinking.

11.

My knowledge of the architecture reveals
I know a little despair
but not the source of the sea smell guiding me
ushering me out into the night air
giving me something to do in this privilege
I've so long tried to ignore, happy
passing time with friends, and even alone.

I toss a paper airplane over the street,
watch its flight into a passing car's open window—
awfully deserving, I think,
of a little applause, so, I'm clapping
when a handsomely dressed couple exit the bar,
pause to register my position, then continue against sirens,
seldom and mixed through a landscape, divided
and mostly out of focus.

12.

Passing by is that me in the future tense?

All these screens emitting light
I'd like to turn away from. The shrugging effect seasons have
when days begin the same, or nearly the same
in gestures, seconds
feelings take to change.

Congratulations on that sweater! I think hear someone say.
Or the other anxieties, different from these

until the question becomes whether or not
the good spells might persist
into areas dark and dangerous that almost belong to me
when the humming of my thoughts
leaves small marks on paper
as I sit between mirrors
when Lindy's not sleeping against the clang
love is
the beginning of a life poetry makes immense.

52 Trees

And what is it that brought you here if not the spell the cedar cast,
beneath which, deer bed on the boughs
of the Pacific Silver fir? The fire willow's new stems
resemble velvet. Addicted to starlings
the sumac shines. Seeds of pitch pine
dream in alder, while cape holly makes excellent cover
for jays building nests out of chinkapin twigs.
The bitter orange shineth, albeit dimly, as though at dusk.
From silver poplar, Donatello sculpted Magdalene.
What does she smell like if not the flowering pear? A saguaro
fulfills an image, but the image
is invisible, like salmon climbing the sitka. The lemon's perfume
mingles with the myrtle in bloom. Living beyond its light
gingko is granted more. The Monterey cypress
is relieved of the burden of fashioning its own form.
Caterpillars populate the hardy catalpa
as the mayten commits to memory the interior dimensions
of the common box. The fig exceeds itself.
A limber pine is in Montana, growing. The olive
waits for it. Jasmine sharpens the hazel's
irregular teeth. The Japanese snowbell sleeps.
But the knockaway's range is limited, and lodgepole pine
is prolific to a fault. The paper birch
examines itself. Branch by branch, ravens dismantle
the Mount Atlas pistachio while an apricot
accuses the hornbeam of murder. Demonstrating poor judgment
quince touch the crown. Ponderosa needles

pierce low clouds. When Thisbe's splashed blood
stains fruit of the mulberry, gray willows become woolly. Lilacs
self-medicate. Twin poplars respond separately
to the same storm. The redwood churns, a towering shrug.
Sycamores go insane. The juniper sways so hard
its roots expand like veins. Ariel howls
inside the live oak. The Pacific yew is so afraid
it grows into a hoop. Taking cues from the copper beech
chestnuts brace. The grand fir falls.
Rarely, the blue palo verde acts like a tree.
The linden is a piece of paper. A paper bird. It is
a woodswallow. In spite of everything
it sings for you. According to the common ash
a person shall be called many things. The eucalyptus
mourns the plum that never released its leaves.

Wind Rings a Bell the Wind Can't Reach

The animal you know throws itself against a mirror.
You leave before the smear.

Your parents are waiting up for you.

You can feel the weight of invisible forces
pressing you into a boy or girl with a taste for leaves,
colors, lines you move within, against
label's threat.
                But you know there is this other world
inside anatomy's swoon,
semi-formal, burning with dissent.

                        •

You whisper to the tree, the tree, the murmuring tree.
You might take action.

Sun melts snow into streams
increasing in volume you control with your lips
around History. Your eyes meet.

Your invisible dress threatens
a slow death. The rest you want to carry, so you listen
to the tree, and its never quite obsolete magic:

•

Touch your mouth

Touch your mouth if it's bleeding
if you didn't see it coming

Be small in the antique hour
in the ambient barb wire

Stand up

Act like a man

Act like a man is the story of fortune

Act like a woman

Act like a woman is the story of woman

Raise your hand

Raise your hand your child

Your child has a dagger, if you don't love her she'll use it

Touch your face

Touch your face there you are

Take off your coat

Take off your shoes your socks

Take off your shirt

Fly into evening's flawed divinity

Land in the tree where the double sex sleeps

Sleep

The invincible summer's inside you

In Light Leaves Collapse

Certain as the end, trees lean toward
the sun, giant in summer

In winter, words surround us

Alive to death

ACKNOWLEDGMENTS

"Nature Breeds a Promise-Keeping Animal" is for Antonio Zambrano-Montes, who was shot and killed by police officers in Pasco, Washington, on February 10, 2015. "Clamor the Bells Falling Bells" borrows its title from Anne Carson's "Lear Town." "Threat Perception" is for Kisha Lewellyn Schlegel. Section 6 of "Threat Perception" is indebted to Mina Loy. Section 10 is indebted to Hilton Als. "52 Trees" is for John Ashbery and is indebted to Lucy Ives, Denis Johnson, and Daniel Mathews. Section 3 of "Wind Rings a Bell the Wind Can't Reach" is indebted to Arthur Rimbaud and Albert Camus.

THANK YOU TO the following editors who first published versions of these poems: Alex Dimitrov at the Academy of American Poets' *Poem-a-Day* for publishing section 7 of "Novella" (previously titled "Were They Hands Would They Flower") and "Wind Rings a Bell the Wind Can't Reach" (previously titled "Evergreen"); Michael Dumanis at *Bennington Review* for publishing section 5 of "Novella" (previously titled "Admittance Fable"); Shane McCrae at *BOAAT* for publishing section 7 of "Clamor the Bells Falling Bells" (previously titled "The Mandrake"); Andrew Nance, Adrienne Raphel, and Christian Schlegel at *Company* for publishing "Early Onset" and "Le Soi"; Zachary Cosby at *Fog Machine* for publishing "Show Cave" (previously titled "Duende Capulets"); Nick Twemlow at *The Iowa Review* for publishing section 8 of "Novella" (previously titled "Sister Wolf"); Alice Bolin at *Okey-Panky* for publishing sections from "Clamor the Bells Falling Bells (previously titled "Lucid Ruse") and "Threat Perception" (previously titled "Lucid Ruse"); Kevin Craft at *Poetry Northwest* for publishing "Nature Breeds a Promise-Keeping Animal"; Robert C. L. Crawford and Stu Watson at *Prelude* for publishing section 6 of "Novella" (previously titled "In a Monstrance of Glass and Topaz") and "Searches"; and India Downes-Le Guin at *Tin House Online* for publishing "Fable on Lunar Formation."

Thank you to everyone at the University of Iowa Press, especially James McCoy, Meredith Stabel, Allison Means, Karen Copp, and Gemma de Choisy.

My deep gratitude to Brenda Shaughnessy, and to Jae Choi, Alan Felsenthal, Emily Kendal Frey, Kate Garklavs, Catie Hannigan, Ally Harris, Erin Howe, Mark Leidner, Dan Poppick, Doug Powell, and Brandon Shimoda.

Kisha, thank you for seeing me how I wish to be seen.

IOWA POETRY PRIZE AND
EDWIN FORD PIPER POETRY AWARD WINNERS

1987
Elton Glaser, *Tropical Depressions*
Michael Pettit, *Cardinal Points*

1988
Bill Knott, *Outremer*
Mary Ruefle, *The Adamant*

1989
Conrad Hilberry, *Sorting the Smoke*
Terese Svoboda, *Laughing Africa*

1990
Philip Dacey, *Night Shift at the Crucifix Factory*
Lynda Hull, *Star Ledger*

1991
Greg Pape, *Sunflower Facing the Sun*
Walter Pavlich, *Running near the End of the World*

1992
Lola Haskins, *Hunger*
Katherine Soniat, *A Shared Life*

1993
Tom Andrews, *The Hemophiliac's Motorcycle*
Michael Heffernan, *Love's Answer*
John Wood, *In Primary Light*

1994
James McKean, *Tree of Heaven*
Bin Ramke, *Massacre of the Innocents*
Ed Roberson, *Voices Cast Out to Talk Us In*

1995
Ralph Burns, *Swamp Candles*
Maureen Seaton, *Furious Cooking*

1996
Pamela Alexander, *Inland*
Gary Gildner, *The Bunker in the Parsley Fields*
John Wood, *The Gates of the Elect Kingdom*

1997
Brendan Galvin, *Hotel Malabar*
Leslie Ullman, *Slow Work through Sand*

1998
Kathleen Peirce, *The Oval Hour*
Bin Ramke, *Wake*
Cole Swensen, *Try*

1999
Larissa Szporluk, *Isolato*
Liz Waldner, *A Point Is That Which Has No Part*

2000
Mary Leader, *The Penultimate Suitor*

2001
Joanna Goodman, *Trace of One*
Karen Volkman, *Spar*

2002
Lesle Lewis, *Small Boat*
Peter Jay Shippy, *Thieves' Latin*

2003
Michele Glazer, *Aggregate of Disturbances*
Dainis Hazners, *(some of) The Adventures of Carlyle, My Imaginary Friend*

2004
Megan Johnson, *The Waiting*
Susan Wheeler, *Ledger*

2005
Emily Rosko, *Raw Goods Inventory*
Joshua Marie Wilkinson, *Lug Your Careless Body out of the Careful Dusk*

2006
Elizabeth Hughey, *Sunday Houses the Sunday House*
Sarah Vap, *American Spikenard*

2008
Andrew Michael Roberts, *something has to happen next*
Zach Savich, *Full Catastrophe Living*

2009
Samuel Amadon, *Like a Sea*
Molly Brodak, *A Little Middle of the Night*

2010
Julie Hanson, *Unbeknownst*
L. S. Klatt, *Cloud of Ink*

2011
Joseph Campana, *Natural Selections*
Kerri Webster, *Grand & Arsenal*

2012
Stephanie Pippin, *The Messenger*

2013
Eric Linsker, *La Far*
Alexandria Peary, *Control Bird Alt Delete*

2014
JoEllen Kwiatek, *[Study for Necessity]*

2015
John Blair, *Playful Song Called Beautiful*
Lindsay Tigue, *System of Ghosts*

2016
Adam Giannelli, *Tremulous Hinge*
Timothy Daniel Welch, *Odd Bloom Seen from Space*

2017
Alicia Mountain, *High Ground Coward*
Lisa Wells, *The Fix*

2018
Rob Schlegel, *In the Tree Where the Double Sex Sleeps*
Cassie Donish, *The Year of the Femme*